Presented to

_____

From

_____

Faith That Does Not Falter

Selections from the writings of

ELISABETH ELLIOT

Fleming H. Revell
A Division of Baker Book House Co
Grand Rapids, Michigan 49516

Published by Fleming H. Revell
a division of Baker Book House Company
P.O. Box 6287, Grand Rapids, MI 49516-6287
www.bakerbooks.com

Printed in Singapore

Library of Congress Cataloging-in-Publication Data
Elliot, Elisabeth.
    Faith that does not falter : selections from the writings of Elisabeth
Elliot / Elisabeth Elliot.
        p.   cm.
    ISBN 0-8007-1819-4
    1. Spiritual life—Christianity. I. Title.
BV4501.3 .E45 2003
248.4—dc21   2002012779

The selections in this book are taken from the following books by Elisabeth Elliot:

All That Was Ever Ours (ATW)   Passion and Purity (PP)
Discipline: The Glad Surrender (D)   Quest for Love (QL)
God's Guidance (GG)   The Mark of a Man (MM)
On Asking God Why (AGW)

Unless otherwise indicated, Scripture references are from *The New English Bible.* Copyright ©1961, 1970, 1989 by The Delegates of Oxford University Press and The Syndics of the Cambridge University Press. Reprinted by permission. Other versions quoted include the King James Version (KJV), the New International Version® NIV® (NIV), the Revised Standard Version (RSV), and the New Testament in Modern English, Revised Edition (PHILLIPS).

Cover photo by George Robinson Studios
Cover and interior design by Robin K. Black

CONTENTS

A Note from the Author   7

FOLLOWING GOD

The Glory of God's Name (GG*)   11

God's Sovereignty, Our Choice (D)   13

Meeting God (AGW)   15

Recognizing Who God Is (GG)   18

How God Works (GG)   20

God's Call (D)   22

Hearing God's Voice (GG)   25

God's Timing (GG)   27

Questioning God (AGW)   30

What to Do with Loneliness (PP)   32

*abbreviation for book title—see copyright page for explanation

LIFE'S MYSTERIES

What Is Faith? (AGW)   37

The Tyranny of Change (ATW)   39

The Mystery of Evil (AGW)   41

Flesh Becomes Word (ATW)   43

The Fellowship of Christ's Suffering (QL)   46

Taking Up Your Cross (GG)   48

The Glad Surrender (D)   50

Matters of the Heart (QL)   55

The Discipline of Waiting (QL)   58

MAKING RIGHT CHOICES

Overcoming Fear (GG)   63

Overcoming Worry (D)   66

Dealing with Doubt (GG)   68

Taking Risks (AGW)   72

The Risks of Witnessing (ATW)   75

Heroes (MM)   78

Choosing the Harder Path (GG)   80

Finding Joy in Work (D)   82

Honoring God with Our Wealth (D)   84

Hope, a Fixed Anchor (ATW)   87

So do not fear, for I am with you;
 do not be dismayed, for I am your God.
I will strengthen you and help you;
 I will uphold you with my righteous right hand.

Isaiah 41:10 niv

A NOTE FROM THE AUTHOR

hat is a Christian supposed to do when terrible things happen? We have two choices—trust God or defy Him. We believe that God is God. He's still got the whole world in His hands and knows exactly what He's doing, or we must believe that He is not God and we are at the awful mercy of mere chance.

Faith is a decision. It is not a deduction from the facts around us. Faith is an act of the will, a choice based on the unbreakable Word of a God who cannot lie, and who showed us what love and obedience and sacrifice mean in the person of Jesus Christ.

The prince of this world approaches. God keeps you from fear, from faltering, and from faithlessness. Remember that the world is watching. What do they see?

ELISABETH ELLIOT

Following God

THE GLORY
OF GOD'S NAME

ld Testament writers made much of the name of God. Israel was a nation specifically set apart as a place for God to put His name. Appeals were made on the basis of the name. "For thy name's sake lead me, and guide me," the psalmist prayed. Not because of who I am, not in recognition of my reputation, but because of who You are. "And his name will be called 'Wonderful Counselor.'" "The Lord is my banner." "Lord God of Hosts." No questions of merit can arise with regard to that name. It is above every name. Therefore I can come today on the ground of that name's merit.

The prayer that Jesus taught His disciples begins with the petition, "Our Father who art in heaven, hallowed be thy name." Whatever our requests may be that bring us to His feet, they should begin with a careful consideration of the meaning of this form of address. If we say the words slowly and thoughtfully, they cannot help but color the rest of the prayer. If it is guidance we are asking, we may be very wrong in our hopes as to the direction it will take. We may be ill-prepared in heart for the road God will choose for us. But, as George MacDonald wrote: "The thought of Him to whom that prayer goes will purify and correct the desire."

> "OUR FATHER WHO ART IN HEAVEN, HALLOWED BE THY NAME."

If we did not have God's unequivocal promise, the words, "Guide *me*, for the sake of *Your* name" would sound outrageously presumptuous. But the truth is that God said He would do just this. There is nothing presumptuous or precarious about it. The validity of the divine word is at stake, and that is a very sure foundation.

GOD'S SOVEREIGNTY,
OUR CHOICE

There are those who do not want to receive Christ. Those who do, however, are given not an "instant kingdom" but the "right to *become* children of God." Here is the truth of divine sovereignty and human responsibility wrapped up in a single verse. To those who *will* He gives. There are many levels of meaning here that we cannot explore. It does not say God makes them instant children of God. It says He gives them the right to become. To those who receive Him, to those who have yielded to Him their allegiance, He gives the right to *become* children of God.

If we hold back our obedience until we have plumbed the theological depths of this mystery, we shall be disobedient. There are truths that cannot be known except by doing them.

13

The Gospels show many cases of those who wished to understand rather than to obey. Jesus had scathing words for them.

On one occasion He turned from them to those who had already believed in Him and said, "If you dwell within the revelation I have brought, you are indeed my disciples; you shall know the truth, and the truth will set *you* free" (John 8:31–32).

TO THOSE WHO WILL HE GIVES.

The Bible does not explain everything necessary for our intellectual satisfaction, but it explains everything necessary for our obedience and hence for God's satisfaction.

MEETING GOD

The Bible is God's message to everybody. We deceive ourselves if we claim to want to hear His voice but neglect the primary channel through which it comes. We must read His Word. We must obey it. We must live it, which means rereading it throughout our lives.

We read that our Heavenly Father actually looks for people who will worship Him in spirit and in reality. Imagine! God is *looking for* worshipers. Will He always have to go to a church to find them, or might there be one here and there in an ordinary house, kneeling alone by a chair, simply adoring Him?

When I stumble out of bed in the morning, put on a robe, and go into my study, words do not spring spontaneously to my lips—other than words like, "Lord, here I am again to talk to You. It's cold. I'm not feeling terribly spiritual." Who can go on and on like that morning after morning, and who can bear to listen to it day after day?

I need help in order to worship God. Nothing helps me more than the Psalms. Here we find human cries—of praise, adoration, anguish, complaint, petition. There is an immediacy, an authenticity, about those cries. They speak for me to God—that is, they say what I often want to say, but for which I cannot find words.

GOD IS LOOKING FOR WORSHIPERS.

Surely the Holy Spirit preserved those Psalms in order that we might have paradigms of prayer and of our individual dealings with God. It is immensely comforting to find that even David, the great king, wailed about his loneliness, his enemies, his pains, his sorrows, and his fears. But then he turned from them to God in paeans of praise.

He found expression for praise far beyond my poor powers, so I use his and am lifted out of myself, up into heights of adoration, even though I'm still the same ordinary woman alone in the same little room.

RECOGNIZING
WHO GOD IS

We have ample evidence that the Lord is able to guide. The promises cover every imaginable situation. All we need to do is take the hand He stretches out. But it is here that the hardest question arises for me. How, exactly, do I take His hand? Isn't this an extreme oversimplification of the conditions of the promises?

I know He has said over and over, "I will guide you." I know the words, "It is the LORD who goes before you; he will be with you, he will not fail you or forsake you; do not fear or be dismayed" (Deut. 31:8 RSV). But there are so many promises with conditions attached, conditions that seem impossible to fulfill for us who are not far along the road to sainthood. Often I have prayed to God for light, and He has shown me some promise in the Bible that indicates He will certainly give me the light I am asking for, *if*—and then I have found, to my despair, that a great deal is asked of me in exchange. Who does God think I am, that I can meet such demands before He will answer my prayer?

The first condition is the recognition of God Himself. It is not who does He think I am, but who do I think He is. I confess that after many years I am still having to go back often to this, to Lesson One in the school of faith. I forget what I learned. I started out on false premises: who I am, what I need, why my case is special, what I'm hoping for, what I pray for, or something— anything but the thing that matters most: who God is.

THE RECOGNITION OF WHO GOD IS IS A LIFETIME PROCESS.

I have called this—the recognition of who God is—the first condition. Perhaps it would be better to call it the primary condition, for it is not one we can fulfill once and for all and then move beyond. The recognition of who God is is a lifetime process. Nor does it end with our earthly life. "This is eternal life, that they know thee the only true God, and Jesus Christ whom thou hast sent" (John 17:3 RSV).

How God Works

When I am looking for the right direction, I ought to take into account what experience I have had, what gifts or propensities are mine, and what the direction of my life heretofore seems to have prepared me for.

It is a scriptural principle that the divine energy acts upon the stuff of this world. Jesus had the servants fill the stone jars that happened to be standing there when He made wine from water at the marriage in Cana. He used a boy's lunch, instead of starting from nothing, to feed five thousand people. His own spittle and the dirt at His feet were the remedies for a blind man's eyes. Common things taken into the divine hands accomplished eternal purposes.

The nature of the thing in question is obviously important. Jesus does not by any means disregard the sort of person we are when He calls us to do His will. He knows our frame and remembers that we are dust. He knows the weaknesses and strengths, the tastes and fears and prejudices and ignorance and experience of each of us. What He wants to make of us, if we are willing to be made over, is sure to bear a relationship to what we are when we first come to Him. It is within His power to transform. It is for us to submit to the transformation.

I have said earlier that God often isolates a man in order to reveal Himself. It is when alone that a man most clearly recognizes God for who He is. But it is in relationship with his fellowmen that he comes to know himself. Seeking the will of God as though it had nothing to do with anybody else leads to all kinds of distortions.

What is in my hand? What is my function in the Body of Christ? Have I something to give? Can I see a place where it is needed now? These questions will help me to know what I ought to do.

JESUS DOES NOT DISREGARD THE SORT OF PERSON WE ARE WHEN HE CALLS US TO DO HIS WILL.

GOD'S CALL

We need never ask the question, "How do I know I'm called?" We ought rather to ask, "How do I know I am *not* called?" We are required to take the risk, move, trust God, make a beginning. This is what Jesus always asked of those who came to Him for help of any kind. Sometimes He asked them to state their case ("What do you want Me to do?"), to affirm their desire ("Do you want to be healed?"), and often to *do* something positive ("Stretch out your hand") before He could do His work. There had to be evidence of faith, some kind of beginning on their part. The first baby step of faith is followed by a daily walk of obedience, and it is as we continue with Him in His Word that we are assured that we were, in fact, called and have nothing to fear.

The most common fear of the true disciple, I suppose, is his own unworthiness. When Paul wrote to the Corinthians, a group

of Christians who had made some terrible messes even inside the church itself, he still never doubted their calling; for they were prepared to hear the Word and to be guided and corrected. It was not the *perfection* of their faith that convinced him they were called. They had made a beginning. In that beginning, Paul found evidence of faith: "It is in full reliance upon God, through Christ, that we make such claims. There is no question of our being qualified in ourselves: we cannot claim anything as our own. The qualification we have comes from God" (2 Cor. 3:4–5).

> WE ARE REQUIRED TO TAKE THE RISK, MOVE, TRUST GOD, MAKE A BEGINNING.

Desire and conviction both play a part in vocation. Often the desire comes first. There may be a natural inclination or an interest aroused by information or perhaps an unexplained longing. If these sometimes-deceptive feelings are offered to the Master and subjected to the test of His Word, they will be confirmed by various means and become a conviction. Sometimes the conviction comes first, accompanied not always by desire but by fear or dread, as in the case of the Old Testament prophets who were given very hard assignments. The only thing to do then is arise and go.

HEARING
GOD'S VOICE

hen Mary went to the garden tomb on the first
Easter morning, she did not know the Lord right
away. She took Him to be the gardener until He spoke her name.
That brought recognition. Instantly she responded, "Master!"
(And we know by those two forms of address, "Mary" and "Master," something important about their relationship.)

In Isaiah we read, "Thus saith the LORD that created thee, . . .
I have called thee by thy name; thou art mine" (43:1 KJV).

How shall we hear that call? Some in our own day have heard
voices, we are told, but I am not one of them. There has never
come to me anything audible. But I have found that the Lord
knows how to call us. (Strange that I should be surprised at that!)
He knows the best way to get our attention, and if we are ready
to listen or to be shown, we will hear or see whatever it is He has
chosen as His means.

THE LORD KNOWS

HOW TO CALL US.

GOD'S TIMING

*I*t is reasonable to expect that God will use whatever means may be appropriate *at the time*. The time I refer to is God's time, not ours. We will know when we need to know, not before.

When I review "all the way which the Lord my God hath led me"—those segments of the way I can remember because they seemed to me significant—I realize that nearly all of my trouble with finding out the will of God came because I wanted it too soon. I like to plan. I like to have things mapped out well in advance, and uncertainty of any sort puts me on edge. Perhaps it is for this very reason God has often asked me to wait until the last minute, right up to what looked like the screaming edge, before I found out what He wanted me to do.

My acceptance of His timing was a rigorous exercise in trust. I was tempted to charge the Lord with negligence and inattention, like the disciples in the boat in a storm. They toiled frantically until the situation became impossible, and then instead of asking for Jesus' help they yelled, "Master, don't you care that we're drowning?" They weren't perishing, they were panicking. It was not too late. Jesus got up and merely spoke to the wind and sea.

On that other occasion, many centuries earlier, when the power of God to command water was what was needed to lead His people, the priests of Israel actually had to get their feet wet before God did anything. Why does He put us to this kind of test? Probably to give us the chance to make a conscious act of faith, often a specific, physical act, a move of some kind toward Him. "And when . . . the feet of the priests bearing the ark were dipped in the brink of the water . . . the waters coming down from above stood and rose up in a heap."

Sometimes we are in a quandary because we have already been shown what we ought to do and we are not satisfied with it. We are saying, "Lord, when are You going to tell me?" and the truth is that He has told us.

Sometimes the word comes very slowly. In Psalm 112:4 we read, "Light rises in the darkness for the upright" (RSV). It may be a gradual thing, imperceptible at first as the coming of the dawn, but long before we see it, the cock crows and there are stirrings. There is no question at all that the dawn will come. We have only to wait.

WE WILL KNOW WHEN
WE NEED TO KNOW,
NOT BEFORE.

QUESTIONING GOD

There are those who insist that it is a very bad thing to question God. To them, "why?" is a rude question. That depends, I believe, on whether it is an honest search, in faith, for His meaning, or whether it is a challenge of unbelief and rebellion. The psalmist often questioned God and so did Job. God did not answer the questions, but He answered the man—with the mystery of Himself.

He has not left us entirely in the dark. We know a great deal more about His purposes than poor old Job did, yet Job trusted Him. He is not only the Almighty—Job's favorite name for Him. He is also our Father, and what a father does is not by any means always understood by the child. If the father loves the child, however, the child trusts him. It is the child's ultimate good that the father has in mind. Terribly elementary. Yet I have to be reminded of this when, for example, my friend suffers, when a book I think I can't possibly do without is lost, when a manuscript is worthless.

In all three I am reminded that God is my Father still, that He does have a purpose for me, and that nothing is useless in the fulfillment of that purpose—if I'll trust Him for it and submit to the lessons.

GOD IS
MY FATHER STILL,
AND HE DOES HAVE
A PURPOSE FOR ME.

What to Do
with Loneliness

e still and know that He is God. When you are
lonely, too much stillness is exactly the thing
that seems to be laying waste your soul. Use the stillness to quiet
your heart before God. Get to know Him. If He is God, He is
still in charge.

Remember that you are not alone. Jesus promised His disciples,
"Lo, I am with you always" (Matt. 28:20). Never mind if you
cannot feel His presence. He is there, never for one moment
forgetting you.

Give thanks. In times of my greatest loneliness I have been
lifted up by the promise of 2 Corinthians 4:17–18, "For this slight
momentary affliction is preparing for us an eternal weight of
glory beyond all comparison, because we look not to the things

that are seen but to the things that are unseen." This is something to thank God for. This loneliness itself, which seems a weight, will be far outweighed by glory.

Refuse self-pity. Refuse it absolutely. It is a deadly thing with power to destroy you. Turn your thoughts to Christ who has already carried your griefs and sorrows.

Accept your loneliness. It is one stage, and only one stage, on a journey that brings you to God. It will not always last.

Offer up your loneliness to God, as the little boy offered to Jesus his five loaves and two fishes. God can transform it for the good of others.

USE THE STILLNESS TO QUIET YOUR HEART BEFORE GOD.

Do something for somebody else. No matter who or where you are, there is something you can do, somebody who needs you. Pray that you may be an instrument of God's peace, that where there is loneliness you may bring joy.

The important thing is to receive this moment's experience with both hands. Don't waste it. "Wherever you are, be all there," Jim once wrote. "Live to the hilt every situation you believe to be the will of God."

Life's Mysteries

WHAT IS FAITH?

r. James I. Packer, in his book *God's Words,* says "The popular idea of faith is of a certain obstinate optimism: the hope, tenaciously held in face of trouble, that the universe is fundamentally friendly and things may get better."

I would have had to be an optimist of the most incorrigible obstinacy to have held on to that sort of faith in the dark times of my own life. It has been another faith that has sustained me— faith in the God of the Bible, a God, as someone once put it, not small enough to be understood but big enough to be worshiped.

If we believe that God is God, our faith is not a deduction from the facts around us. It is not an instinct. It is not inferred from the happy way things work. Faith is a gift from God, and we must respond to Him with a decision: The God of the universe has spoken, we believe what He says, and we will obey. We must make a decision that we will hold in the face of all opposition and apparent contradiction.

THE GOD OF THE UNIVERSE HAS SPOKEN, WE BELIEVE WHAT HE SAYS, AND WE WILL OBEY.

The powers of hell can never prevail against the soul that takes its stand on God and on His Word. This kind of faith overcomes the world. The world of today must be shown. We (you and I) must show people what Jesus showed the world on that dark day so long ago—that we love the Father and will do what He says.

THE TYRANNY
OF CHANGE

There are many things we want to be liberated from, many kinds of tyranny from which we would like to escape, but one of the inescapable ones is the tyranny of change. (I didn't make up that idea. I got it from Paul, reading the Phillips' translation of Romans 8:20–21.)

Most of us are ambivalent about change. We say, "Let's do this for a change," and in the next breath moan, "Oh dear, how things have changed! They're just not the same anymore." Lots of people do things purely for the sake of doing something different. And one of the ironies is that things don't necessarily turn out to be all that fresh and original after all.

I don't like change very much. I am not always moving the furniture around. I don't want any "bright new taste surprises" for breakfast. I want the sofa where it was yesterday and the black coffee just the way I always make it.

> THERE ARE ENOUGH CHANGES WE CANNOT STOP, WHICH ARE MEANT TO DRIVE US TO GOD.

It was reassuring to me to learn that C. S. Lewis also liked monotony and routine. Urged time and again to journey abroad to lecture, he stayed home and smoked his pipe and lectured where he felt he belonged. He also wrote wonderful things and remained content with familiar surroundings, able to draw on deep inner resources.

We need not be always seeking something different, something other, out of mere restlessness. There are enough changes we cannot stop, which are of the essence of this life and are meant to be. They are meant to drive us to God.

The world of creation, said Paul, has, in God's purpose, been given hope. "And the hope is that in the end the whole of created life will be rescued from the tyranny of change and decay, and have its share in that magnificent liberty which can only belong to the children of God."

THE MYSTERY OF EVIL

Evil men have often been permitted to do what they please. We must understand that divine permission is given for evil to work. To know the God of the Bible is to see that He who could have made automatons of all of us made instead free creatures with power and permission to defy Him.

There is a limit, of course. Let us not forget this. The Tower of Babel was stopped. God has set limits on what man is allowed to do, but one day He put Himself into men's hands. Jesus had sat in the temple teaching and nobody touched Him, but the time came when the same people who had listened to Him barged into Gethsemane with swords and cudgels. Jesus did not flee. He walked straight up to them. He was unconcerned about physical safety. His only safety was the will of the Father. "This is your moment," He said, "the hour when darkness reigns" (Luke 22:53).

Why did God make room for that moment? Why should there ever be an hour when darkness is free to rule?

When Jesus refused to answer Pilate the next morning, Pilate said, "Surely you know that I have authority to release you, and I have authority to crucify you." Jesus' reply embraces the mystery of evil: "You would have no authority at all over me if it had not been granted you from above" (John 19:10–11).

"YOU WOULD HAVE NO AUTHORITY AT ALL OVER ME IF IT HAD NOT BEEN GRANTED YOU FROM ABOVE."

Every man and woman who chooses to trust and obey God will find his or her faith attacked and life invaded by the power of evil. There is no more escape for us than there was for the Son of Man. The way Jesus walked is the way we must walk.

FLESH BECOMES WORD

ords are inadequate, we say. So they often are. But they are nonetheless precious. "A word fitly spoken is like apples of gold in pictures of silver." In a time of crisis we learn how intensely we need both flesh and word. We cannot do well without either one. The bodily presence of people we love is greatly comforting, and their silent companionship blesses us. "I know I can't say anything that will help, but I wanted to come," someone says, and the word they would like to speak is spoken by their coming. Those who can't come send, instead of their presence, word. A letter comes, often beginning, "I don't know what to say," but it is an expression, however inadequate, of the person himself and what he feels toward us.

Before Eve heard the voice of the serpent summoning her to the worst possibility of her being, before Adam heard the voice of God summoning him to his best, the Word was. The Word was

at the beginning of things, the Word was with God, the Word was God. That Word became visible in the flesh when the man Christ came to earth. Man saw Him, talked with Him, learned from Him, and when His flesh was glorified and He returned once more to His Father, men declared what they had seen. "That which was from the beginning, which we have heard, which we have seen with our eyes, which we have looked upon and touched with our hands, concerning the word of life ... we proclaim also to you" (I John 1:1, 3 RSV). That eternal Word had become flesh, and through those who knew Christ that flesh had become once

THAT ETERNAL WORD HAD BECOME FLESH, AND THROUGH THOSE WHO KNEW CHRIST THAT FLESH HAD BECOME ONCE MORE WORD.

more Word. Those who hear that Word today and believe it begin to live it, and again it becomes flesh.

THE FELLOWSHIP
OF CHRIST'S SUFFERING

n this world," Jesus said, "you will have trouble. But take heart! I have overcome the world" (John 16:33 NIV). None of us likes pain. All of us wish at times that we need not "go through all this stuff." Let's settle it once and for all: We cannot know Christ and the power of His resurrection without the fellowship of His suffering.

Often with that thought arises another: Can *my* sufferings have anything to do with His? Because my fickle feelings bring turmoil and sorrow in my life, can I nevertheless hope for some small share in that divine fellowship? The apostle Paul helps us here. He had known many kinds of severe suffering that were directly related to his work for God (and few of our afflictions, I suppose, would fall into *that* category), yet even he says, "Forgetting what is behind and

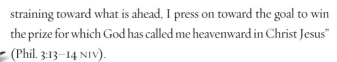

straining toward what is ahead, I press on toward the goal to win the prize for which God has called me heavenward in Christ Jesus" (Phil. 3:13–14 NIV).

By the grace of God, we can will to do His will. Forget the past. Press toward the goal.

WE CANNOT KNOW CHRIST
AND THE POWER
OF HIS RESURRECTION
WITHOUT THE FELLOWSHIP
OF HIS SUFFERING.

TAKING UP YOUR CROSS

All our problems are theological ones, William Temple said. All of them have to do with our relationship to God and His to us, and this is precisely why it makes sense to come to God with them.

The taking up of the cross will mean sooner or later saying no to self. But it is also a resounding yes. It means saying yes when everything in us says no. To decide to do the thing that we (and, it will seem, everybody else in the world) do not want to do because it is not "natural." And in our giving of wholehearted assent, we find to our amazement that the impossible becomes possible and the things we were sure were beyond us are now within reach, for God's command is His enabling. *Never* has He given an assignment that was not accompanied by the power to accomplish it.

The cross entails sacrifice, too. There is no getting around this. Christianity has been criticized and rejected by many as an "unnatural" religion, a life that denies living, a negation and not an affirmation. Jesus never tried to make it look easy. The principles He taught cut across the grain of human nature: lose your life in order to find it; be poor in spirit if you want to be happy; mourn if you want to rejoice; take the last place if you want the first. The corn of wheat must first fall into the ground and die if it is ever to produce anything.

WHAT WE MUST NOT FORGET IS THAT JESUS TRAVELED THIS ROAD BEFORE US.

What we must not forget is that He traveled this road before us. "He himself endured a cross and thought nothing of its shame"—not because He had a particular liking for self-denial and suffering but "because of the joy he knew would follow his suffering. ...Think constantly of him enduring all that sinful men could say against him, and you will not lose your purpose or your courage" (Heb. 12:2–3 PHILLIPS).

The Glad Surrender

As a child in a Christian home, I did not start out with an understanding of the word *discipline*. I simply knew that I belonged to people who loved me and cared for me. That is dependence. They spoke to me, and I answered. That is responsibility. They gave me things to do, and I did them. That is obedience. It adds up to discipline. In other words, the totality of the believer's response is discipline.

While there are instances where the words *discipline* and *obedience* seem to be interchangeable, I am using the first as comprehending the second and always presupposing both dependence and responsibility. We might say that discipline is the disciple's "career." It defines the very shape of the disciple's life. Obedience, on the other hand, refers to specific action.

Discipline is the believer's answer to God's call. It is the recognition, not of the solution to his problems or the supply of his

needs, but of mastery. God addresses us. We are responsible—
that is, we must make a response. We may choose to say yes and
thus fulfill the Creator's glorious purpose for us, or we may say
no and violate it. This is what is meant by moral responsibility.
God calls us to freedom, fulfillment, and joy—but we can refuse
them. In a deep mystery, hidden in God's purposes for man
before the foundation of the world, lies the truth of man's
free will and God's sovereignty.

> DISCIPLINE
> IS THE
> WHOLEHEARTED
> YES TO THE
> CALL OF GOD.

This much we know: A God who is sovereign chose to create a man capable of willing his own freedom and therefore capable of answering the call.

Jesus, in response to the will of the Father, demonstrated what it means to be fully human when He took upon Himself the form of a man and in so doing voluntarily and gladly chose both dependence and obedience. Humanity for us, as for Christ, means both dependence and obedience.

The unwillingness on the part of men and women to acknowledge their helpless dependence is a violation of our "creature-liness." The unwillingness to be obedient is a violation of our humanity. Both are declarations of independence and, whether physical or moral, are essentially atheistic. In both, the answer to the call is no.

Discipline is the wholehearted yes to the call of God. When I know myself called, summoned, addressed, taken possession of, known, acted upon, I have heard the Master. I put myself gladly, fully, and forever at His disposal, and to whatever He says my answer is yes.

Matters
of the Heart

earts do break. The same hearts are breakable over and over again.

Is there anywhere to turn but to Him who "heals the broken-hearted and binds up their wounds" (Ps. 147:3 NIV)? Broken hearts are not new to Him, and His power is limitless, for He is the One who numbers the stars and calls them all by name (v. 4). Have you noticed these two verses that juxtapose God's concern for the wounded *and* His numbering and naming the stars? His compassion and His power are mentioned together that we might understand that the Lord of the Universe is not so preoccupied with the galaxies that He cannot stoop to minister to our sufferings.

He has a glorious purpose in permitting the heartbreak. We find many clues for this in Scripture. For example:

OUR SMALL
HURTS,
SO INFINITELY
SMALLER
THAN HIS,
MAY YET
BE TRUSTFULLY
SURRENDERED
TO HIS
TRANSFORMING
WORK.

that we may be shaped to the likeness of Christ (Rom. 8:29)

that we may learn to trust (2 Cor. 1:8–9)

that we may learn to obey (Ps. 119:67, 71)

that we may bear fruit (John 15:2)

that we may reach spiritual maturity (James 1:4)

Our sufferings are not for nothing. Never. However small they may be, we may see them as God's mercy in giving us the chance to unite them with His own sufferings. Christ suffered for our sins and we suffer because of the sins of others (and they suffer because of ours). There is a mystery here, far deeper than our understanding, but we may take it on faith, on the authority of the Word, and believe it will not go for nothing.

A broken heart is an acceptable offering to God. He will never despise it. We do not know what unimagined good He can bring about through our simple offering. Christ was willing to be broken bread for the life of the world. He was poured out like wine. This means He accepted being ground like wheat and crushed like the grape. It was the hands of others who did the grinding and crushing. Our small hurts, so infinitely smaller than His, may yet be trustfully surrendered to His transforming work. The trial of faith is a thing worth much more than gold.

THE DISCIPLINE
OF WAITING

*I*s there a harder discipline than that of waiting, especially when one's desires seem as wild and uncontrollable as a prairie fire?

Without real trust in who God is—trust in His never-failing love and wisdom, we set ourselves up for disappointment. Is He a good God? Will He give what is best? If the answer is yes to both questions, it follows that He will withhold many things that look attractive to us. It is His mercy to withhold them. Shall we accuse Him of failure to get "His act" together or shall we echo the psalmist's word, "I am still confident of this: I will see the goodness of the LORD in the land of the living. Wait for the LORD; be strong and take heart and wait for the LORD" (Ps. 27:13–14 NIV).

If we imagine that happiness is to be found by furious pursuit, we will end up in a rage at the unsatisfying results. If, on the other hand, we set ourselves to pursue the wise and loving and holy will of our Heavenly Father, we will find that happiness comes—quietly, in unexpected ways, and surprisingly often, as the by-product of *sacrifice*.

GOD IS IN THE WAITING.

Waiting is a form of suffering—the difficulty of self-restraint, the anguish of unfulfilled longing, the bewilderment of unanswered prayer, flesh and heart failing, soul breaking. These are indeed tribulations, and tribulation is the curriculum if we are to learn patience. We want answers *now*, right *now*, but we are required at times to walk in darkness.

Nevertheless, God is in the darkness.

"My soul, wait thou only upon God; for my expectation is from him" (Ps. 62:5 KJV). In Him alone lie our security, our confidence, our trust. A spirit of restlessness and resistance can never wait, but one who believes he is loved with an everlasting love and knows that underneath are the everlasting arms will find strength and peace.

God is in the waiting.

Making Right Choices

OVERCOMING FEAR

One particular spot where I lived as a missionary became like a "place of dragons." It was full of things I was afraid of and did not know how to cope with. Once in a while I felt as though I were about to be devoured. "Sore broken" is the psalmist's expression, and I thought I knew how he felt. I was on my way back to that place one night, camping where we usually did at the junction of two rivers. The Indians had made me a reed hut to sleep in and had finished their own hut-building, fishing, eating, and talking. Everything was quiet except for the night birds and tree frogs. There was nothing especially distinct about this journey back home. I had made it before.

IF WE BEAR IN MIND
THAT WE SHALL
FINALLY DWELL
IN THE HOUSE
OF THE LORD, THEN
THE INTERMEDIATE
PASTURES AND WATERS,
EVEN THE VALLEY
OF THE SHADOW OR
THE PLACE OF DRAGONS,
ARE UNDERSTOOD.

But as I lay in my blanket I began to feel something like what fell on Abraham: "a horror of great darkness." How could I go back to those "dragons"? My heart was about to turn back.

Then I thought of Jesus' words to His disciples: "Lo, I am with you all the days." If He was with me then I was certainly with Him. The place of dragons was the place He was taking me, and I was still following—I had not gotten off the track. I was with Him still, sharing in a small measure His cross.

Never for a second does God lose sight of His objective. It is we who forget what it is. We are distracted by immediate circumstances, and it is no wonder we want to give up the whole thing. It was the "joy that was set before Him" that enabled Jesus to endure the cross.

Without a clear understanding of the ultimate objective, the intermediate objectives make no sense to us. "Why this, Lord?" we keep asking. But if we bear in mind that we shall, beyond any doubt whatsoever, finally dwell in the house of the Lord, settle down to stay in His presence, then the intermediate pastures and waters, even the valley of the shadow or the place of dragons, are understood. They are stations and landings along the journey, and they will not last long.

Overcoming Worry

*F*rustration is not the will of God. Of that we can be quite certain. There is time to do anything and everything that God wants us to do. Obedience fits smoothly into His given framework. One thing that most certainly will not fit into it is worry. Here are six reasons why:

1. Worry is totally fruitless. Have you ever succeeded in adding an inch where you wanted it, or subtracting one where you didn't want it, merely by being anxious? If you can't accomplish that by worrying, what *can* you accomplish?

2. Worry is worse than fruitless: it is disobedience. Note these commands: Fret not; fear not; let not your hearts be troubled; be not dismayed; be of good cheer.

3. Worry is taking the not-given—for example, tomorrow. We are allowed to plan for tomorrow, but we are not

allowed to worry about it. Today's troubles are enough of a burden. Jesus knew exactly what He was talking about when He said that.

4. Worry is refusing the given. Today's care, not tomorrow's, is the responsibility given to us, apportioned in the wisdom of God. Often we neglect the

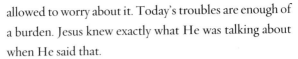

WORRY IS THE ANTITHESIS OF TRUST.

thing assigned for the moment because we are preoccupied with something that is not our business just now. How easy it is to give only half our attention to someone who needs us—friend, husband, or little child—because the other half is focused on a future worry.

5. Worry is the antithesis of trust. You simply cannot do both. They are mutually exclusive.

6. Worry is a wicked squandering of time (as well as energy).

Direct your time and energy into worry, and you will be deficient in things like singing with grace in your heart, praying with thanksgiving, listening to a child's account of his school day, inviting a lonely person to supper, sitting down to talk unhurriedly with wife or husband, writing a note to someone who needs it.

DEALING WITH DOUBT

"Be still, and know that I am God."

If we have once kept silent long enough to know this, we have, at least in that moment, been ready to obey. But it is the being still that is so hard for us. It often takes illness, loss, suffering of some kind, isolation, and loneliness. Only when we have come to the end of our own resources, when few distractions are left to us, does it become possible to be quiet.

But if, in the providence of God, we have not yet had to weather a real crisis, we may "be still" on purpose. We may choose to obey the command, stop all activity, turn aside in stillness, and know. The best kind of beginning, when we are wanting to know the will of God, is to concentrate first on God Himself. And of course, the briefest effort to do this will humble us, for we will learn how poorly we are in control of our thoughts. For me, there is nothing like the printed word to help me corral my scattered thoughts.

THE BEST KIND
OF BEGINNING, WHEN WE
ARE WANTING TO KNOW
THE WILL OF GOD, IS
TO CONCENTRATE FIRST
ON GOD HIMSELF.

Simply looking at a verse in the Bible that tells me something of God and reading through a hymn or a prayer are aids to discipline, and I need all the aids I can get.

I have been told that in one of the China Inland Mission homes in China there was a motto on the wall that said, "The sun stood still. The iron did swim. This God is our God for ever and ever. He will be our guide even unto death." This God, the One who, in answer to the prayer of an ordinary man, stopped the sun in its course, the God who suspended His own law of gravity and made an ax head float, this is the God to whom I come. This is the God whose will and direction I am asking. This God is the One whose promises I am counting on. Whatever my predicament may be, as soon as I compare it with the circumstances surrounding the miracles of the sun and the ax, my doubts seem comical.

God knows all about those comical doubts. He knows our frame. He remembers that we are dust, and it is to us, knowing all this better than we know it ourselves, that He made those promises.

God is, according to Isaiah 43, our Creator, our Redeemer, the Lord our God, the Holy One of Israel, our Savior. Would we ask Him to be anything more than this, before we admit in our hearts that He can be trusted?

Taking Risks

An ancient longing for danger, for challenge, and for sacrifice stirs in us. We have been insulated from having to watch others suffer by putting them where somebody else will do the watching and from guilt by calling any old immorality a "new morality." We don't risk involvement if we can help it. We try not to turn around if somebody screams. Responsibility for others we'd rather delegate to institutions, including the government, which are supposed to make it their business to handle it.

I saw a man on television telling us that what America needs is a little more honesty. Because of technology, the man said, people have to be more dependent on each other than they used to be (Oh?) and therefore we need more honesty (Oh). Probably, he allowed, our standards have never been quite what they ought to be and it's time to hike them up a notch or two.

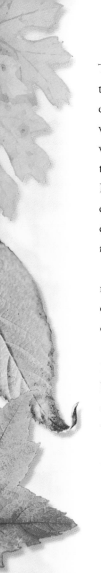

How do we go about this? Take a deep breath and—all together now—start being honest? Ah, the man had a plan. I waited, tense and eager, to hear what it might be. Popularization was what he proposed. Make honesty the In Thing. If everybody's doing it, it will be easy. In fact, it would take the *risk* out of it.

JESUS CALLS US STILL TO FOLLOW HIM: "LET A MAN DENY HIMSELF AND TAKE UP HIS CROSS."

Funny, I always thought righteousness was supposed to be risky. I was taught it wasn't easy, and I found it hard when I tried it. It's never likely to be either easy or popular.

I'm for civilization. I'm all for certain kinds of progress and I accept quite gladly most of today's means of avoiding the risks, but to imagine that we shall whip off the dishonesty that is characteristic of fallen human nature everywhere as painlessly as we whip off one garment and put on another, to imagine that by simply taking a different view we shall come up with a no-risk brand of honesty, is a piece of self-deception and fatuity to make the mind reel.

Plato, three hundred years before Christ, predicted that if ever the truly good man were to appear, the man who would tell the truth, he would have his eyes gouged out and in the end be crucified.

That risk was once taken, in its fullest measure. The man appeared. He told the world the truth about itself and even made the preposterous claim "I am the Truth." As Plato foresaw, that man was crucified.

He calls us still to follow Him, and the conditions are the same: "Let a man deny himself and take up his cross."

THE RISKS OF WITNESSING

itnessing means obedience. Every time you do what God says to do or refuse to do what He says not to do you witness to the truth. And witnessing to the truth is a very risky business—risky in the world's terms. You're likely to be arrested, Jesus predicted, handed over to prison, brought before governors and kings. Aleksandr Solzhenitsyn, Dietrich Bonhoeffer, Corrie ten Boom, and thousands of others knew what He meant. They also understood what He said next: "Hold on, and you will win your souls. In the world you'll have tribulation, but cheer up, I have overcome the world."

Witnessing conquers the world, but it doesn't exempt you from suffering. Witness enables others to see what they could not otherwise have seen. It changes the picture. Think of Stephen. He never minced any words. Standing before the highest civil

and religious court of the Jewish nation, called the Sanhedrin, he witnessed. He spoke the plain truth about Israel's history.

If miracles didn't persuade them, what would Stephen's defiance do? They ground their teeth at him in a rage and stoned him to death. But while the rocks were flying, Stephen saw something. He saw heaven opened, he saw the glory of God and Jesus Himself standing at His right hand. That's witness. It conquers the world. It makes truth visible. It changes the picture.

When we see Stephen we see not the fury of the religious Jews, not the rain of stones falling on his head, but a man

FAITH STANDS IN THE MIDST OF SUFFERING AND SEES GLORY.

beholding the Lord. Faith stands in the midst of suffering and sees glory. The Church is here not to deliver us from suffering. The Church will make witnesses, those who see the promises of God, the angel in the lions' den, the Son of Man in the flames, Jesus standing up to welcome His beloved Stephen.

HEROES

Of the many young people who tell me that Jim Elliot's life has inspired their lives, it is surprising how many carefully preface their remarks with disclaimers such as, "I don't mean he's a hero or anything."

Well, what is a hero, anyway? "Any man admired for his courage, nobility, or exploits, the central figure in any important event, honored for outstanding qualities." Wasn't Jim a hero? We badly need heroes. How else shall we grasp the meaning of courage or strength or holiness? We need to see such truth made visible in the lives of human beings, and Jim did that, it seems to me.

Heroes are paradigms. They show us what strength or courage or purity actually *looks* like. Jesus was a hero in that sense. Consider His last night before the Crucifixion. After praying the great prayer of John 17 He had gone with the disciples to the

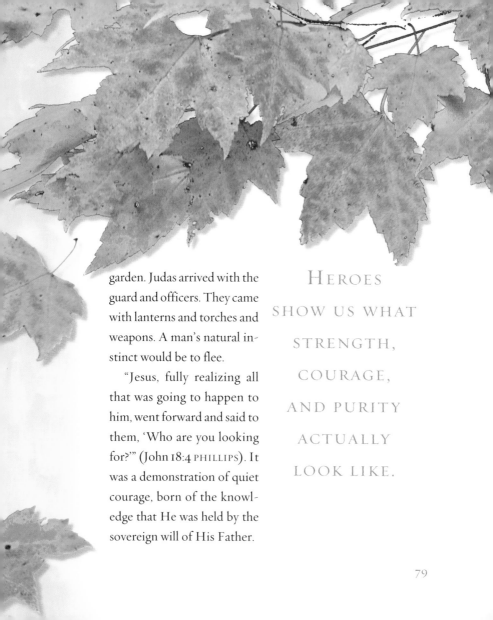

garden. Judas arrived with the guard and officers. They came with lanterns and torches and weapons. A man's natural instinct would be to flee.

"Jesus, fully realizing all that was going to happen to him, went forward and said to them, 'Who are you looking for?'" (John 18:4 PHILLIPS). It was a demonstration of quiet courage, born of the knowledge that He was held by the sovereign will of His Father.

HEROES SHOW US WHAT STRENGTH, COURAGE, AND PURITY ACTUALLY LOOK LIKE.

CHOOSING
THE HARDER PATH

Most of us avoid crises when we can. It is far more comfortable to sit in the back row than to stand up and be counted. To take up the cross and follow, to walk in the light, to climb "the steep ascent of heaven" are not options that have a strong popular appeal.

But we are speaking of those who actually want to do the will of God. What we are concerned with now is the business of choice when both alternatives seem equally moral.

Choose the harder of the two ways. If you have eliminated all other possibilities and there still seem to be two that might please God, choose the more difficult one. "The way is hard, that leads to life," Jesus said, so it is likely that He is asking us to will against our will.

But what if He isn't asking that? The more sincerely we seek the will of God, the more fearful we will be that we may miss it. If it made little difference to us, obviously we would not worry very much about it, so there ought to be a measure of reassurance for us in the very fact of our fear. Jesus is in the boat with us, no matter how wild the storm is, and He is at peace. He commands us not to be afraid.

JESUS IS IN THE BOAT WITH US, NO MATTER HOW WILD THE STORM IS, AND HE IS AT PEACE.

The supreme example, outside that of our Lord Himself, of a man willing against his own will, in obedience to God, is Abraham. He was asked to sacrifice Isaac, his only son—and this, in the face of all God's promises about descendants. Abraham was to tie the boy down on top of a pile of kindling on an altar. This he did (with what anguish we can only imagine), and only then, when with the knife poised he had triumphantly passed the hardest test of faith, did God show him that his son's death was not finally required.

FINDING JOY IN WORK

The Christian attitude toward work is truly revolutionary. Think what it would do to the economy and the entire fabric of life if the question were asked daily: "Who is your Master?" and the answer were given: "Christ is my Master, whose slave I am." It would transform in a stroke not only the worker's attitude toward the boss, but his attitude toward those who work with him. He would not be seeking ways to evade work that he doesn't like. It would change his attitude toward the work itself because he would do it with single-mindedness, for Christ. It would change the quality of the work, for he has a master who sees every detail of the work done and the intentions of the heart.

Think of the brightness there will be in the place where work is done for God. Think of the peace in the heart of the workman who lifts it up to Him. We will finish our course with joy if we stick to the assignment. We will be able to say as Jesus did, "I have finished the work you gave me."

THINK OF THE BRIGHTNESS
THERE WILL BE IN THE PLACE
WHERE WORK IS DONE FOR GOD.

Honoring God
with Our Wealth

*F*ew of us are well acquainted with the extremes that the apostle Paul knew: "I know what it is to be brought low, and I know what it is to have plenty. I have been very thoroughly initiated into the human lot with all its ups and downs, fullness and hunger, plenty and want." In whatever measure we have experienced these, the Lord has given us opportunity to learn the vital disciplines of possessions.

The first lesson is that things are *given by God*. "He did not spare his own Son, but gave him up for us all; and with this gift how can he fail to lavish upon us all he has to give?" (Rom. 8:32).

The second lesson is that things are given us *to be received with thanksgiving*. Faith looks up with open hands. "You are giving me this, Lord? Thank you. It is good and acceptable and perfect."

The third lesson is that things can be *material for sacrifice*. This is what is called the eucharistic life. The Father pours out His blessings on us; we receive them with open hands, give thanks, and lift them up as an offering back to Him, thus completing the circle.

This lesson leads naturally to the fourth, which is that things are given to us *to enjoy for a while*.

Nothing has done more damage to the Christian view of life than the hideous notion that those who are truly spiritual have lost all interest in this world and its beauties. The Bible says, "God ... endows us richly with all things to enjoy." It also says, "Do not set your hearts on the godless world or anything in it." It is altogether fitting and proper that we should enjoy things made for us to enjoy. What is not at all fitting or proper is that we should set our hearts on them. Temporal things must be treated as temporal

TEMPORAL THINGS MUST BE RECEIVED, GIVEN THANKS FOR, OFFERED BACK, AND *ENJOYED*. THEY MUST NOT BE TREATED LIKE ETERNAL THINGS.

things—received, given thanks for, offered back, but *enjoyed.* They must not be treated like eternal things.

And there is a fifth lesson: *All that belongs to Christ is ours.* As Amy Carmichael wrote, "All that was ever ours is ours forever."

We often say that what is ours belongs to Christ. Do we remember the opposite: that what is His is ours? That seems to me a wonderful truth, almost an incredible truth. If it is so, how can we really "lose" anything? How can we even speak of His having the "right" to *our* possessions?

"Son, thou art ever with me, and all that I have is thine," the Father says to us. That is riches.

HOPE, A FIXED ANCHOR

Christian hope is a different sort of thing from other kinds. The real essence of the word is *trust*.

When Lazarus died, the hopes of his two loving sisters, Mary and Martha, were dashed. Jesus, hearing the news, did not hurry to the house but stayed where He was for two more days. When He finally got to Bethany both sisters greeted Him with the same words: "If only You had been here, Lord!"

Jesus said, "I Myself am the resurrection." This is our hope. It is a living thing. It is, in fact, Christ Himself. It is also something to live by. When our hopes for healing or success or the solution to a problem or freedom from financial distress seem to come to nothing, we feel just as Mary and Martha did. Jesus might have done something about it, but He didn't. We lie awake thinking about all the "if onlys." We wonder if it is somehow our fault that the thing didn't work. We doubt whether prayer is of any use after all. Is God up there? Is He listening? Does He care?

Mary and Martha had envisioned His coming and raising a sick man from his bed. He came too late. Unfortunately Lazarus

IF I BELIEVE, TRUST,
FLEE TO GOD FOR REFUGE,
I AM SAFE EVEN IN MY SORROW,
HELD BY THE CONFIDENCE
OF GOD'S UTTER
TRUSTWORTHINESS.

was dead—so dead, Martha pointed out, that decomposition would have set in. It had not crossed their minds that they were about to see an even more astonishing thing than the one they had hoped for—a swaddled corpse answering the Master's call and walking, bound and muffled, out of the tomb.

The truth of the story is that God knew what was happening. Nothing was separating the grieving women from His love. He heard their prayers, counted their tears, held His peace. *But He was faithful, and He was at work.* He had a grand miracle in mind.

The duration of my suffering may be longer than that of Lazarus's sisters, but if I believe, trust, flee to God for refuge, I am safe even in my sorrow. I am held by the confidence of God's utter trustworthiness. He is at work, producing miracles I haven't imagined. I must wait for them.

Elisabeth Elliot is a popular seminar speaker, radio teacher, and best-selling author. Her books include *A Chance to Die, On Asking God Why, The Journals of Jim Elliot, The Mark of a Man,* and *Discipline: The Glad Surrender.*